# How to Draw Kawaii Manga
# FASHION

**Quarto.com**
**WalterFoster.com**

First Published in 2024 by Walter Foster Publishing, an imprint of The Quarto Group,
100 Cummings Center, Suite 265-D, Beverly, MA 01915, USA.
T (978) 282-9590 F (978) 283-2742

Walter Foster Publishing titles are also available at discount for retail, wholesale,
promotional, and bulk purchase. For details, contact the Special Sales Manager by
email at specialsales@quarto.com or by mail at The Quarto Group, Attn: Special
Sales Manager, 100 Cummings Center, Suite 265-D, Beverly, MA 01915, USA.

28 27 26 25 24      1 2 3 4 5

ISBN: 978-0-7603-8871-6

Digital edition published in 2024
eISBN: 978-0-7603-8872-3

Library of Congress Control Number is available

Design: Cindy Samargia Laun
Illustration: Misako Rocks!

Printed in China

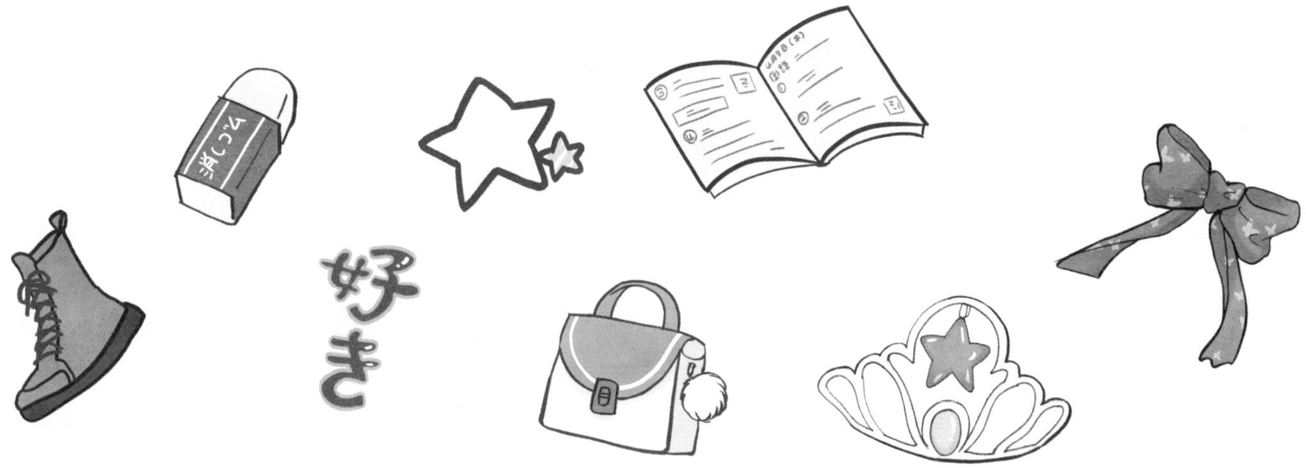
好き

# CONTENTS

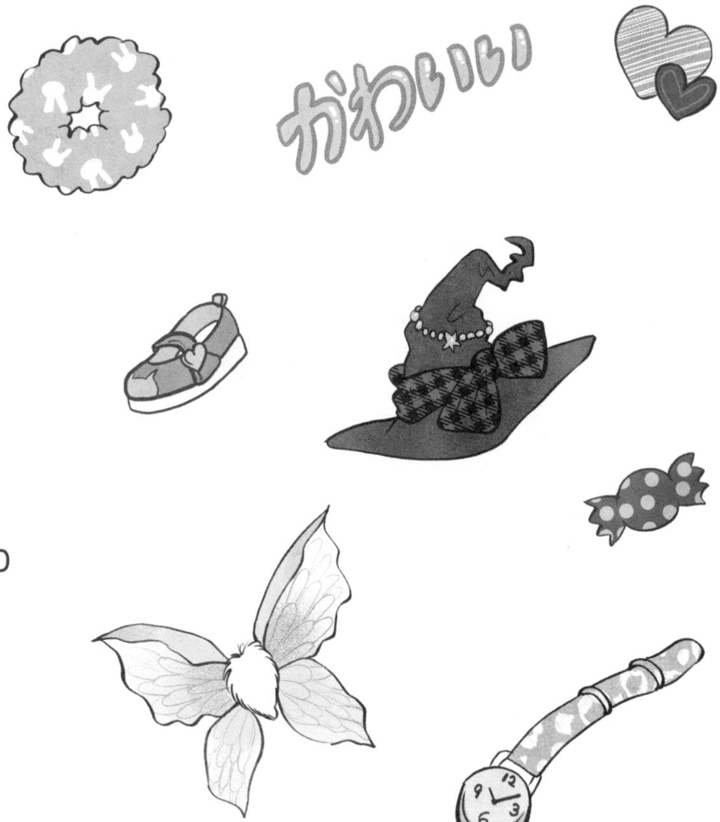
かわいい



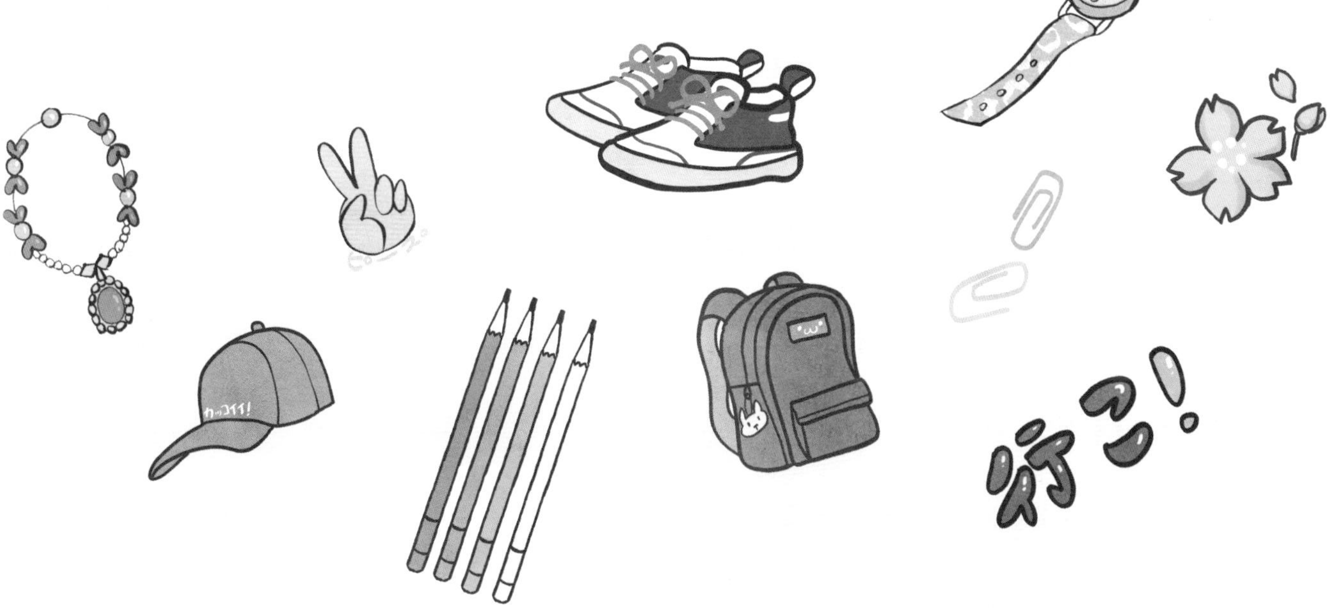
行こ!

# INTRODUCTION

This book is for anyone who loves kawaii "cute" things and wants to learn to draw in a manga and anime drawing style with a bubbly and positive attitude! Don't be afraid to try. You will gain confidence in your drawing abilities as you follow along with each lesson.

行こ! LET'S GO!

スクール SCHOOL

プリティ PRETTY

トゥウィーン TWEEN

ティーン TEEN

描こ LET'S DRAW!

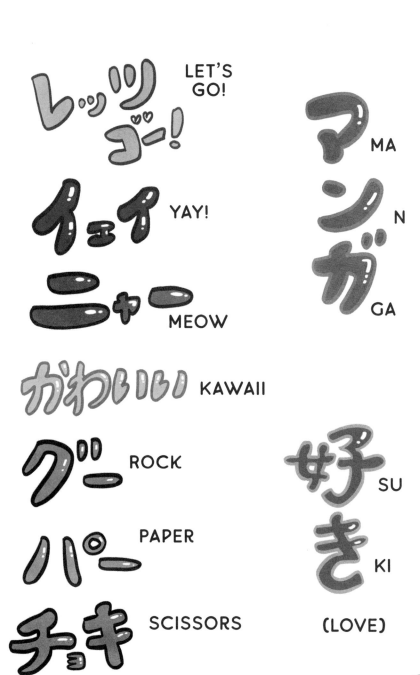

レッツゴー! LET'S GO!

イェイ YAY!

ニャー MEOW

かわいい KAWAII

グー ROCK

パー PAPER

チョキ SCISSORS

マンガ MA N GA

好き SU KI (LOVE)

# Manga Drawing Tools

SKETCHBOOK

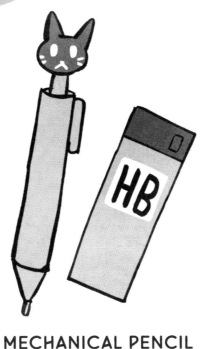

MECHANICAL PENCIL

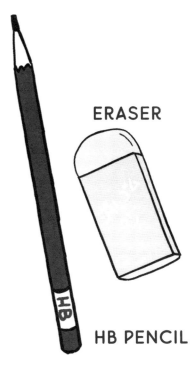

ERASER

HB PENCIL

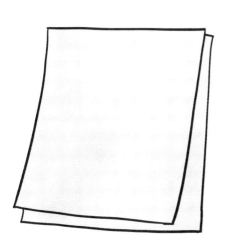

TRACING PAPER
AND DRAWING
PAPER

COLORED
PENCILS

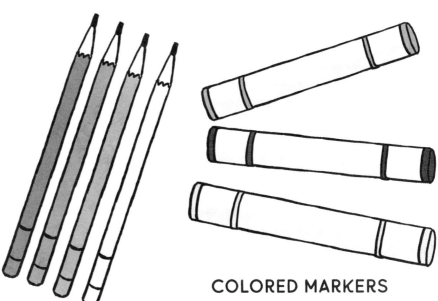

COLORED MARKERS

**Misako's note:**
There are many fun and useful materials to choose from. Try using various brands to find your favorite. You can use tracing paper to help you practice drawing. Have fun with it!

# GETTING STARTED
## Manga faces & bodies start with guidelines.

**Misako's note:** I totally understand if you like to start drawing clothes right away because I'm like you. But guidelines really help us draw different angles of the body and outfits!

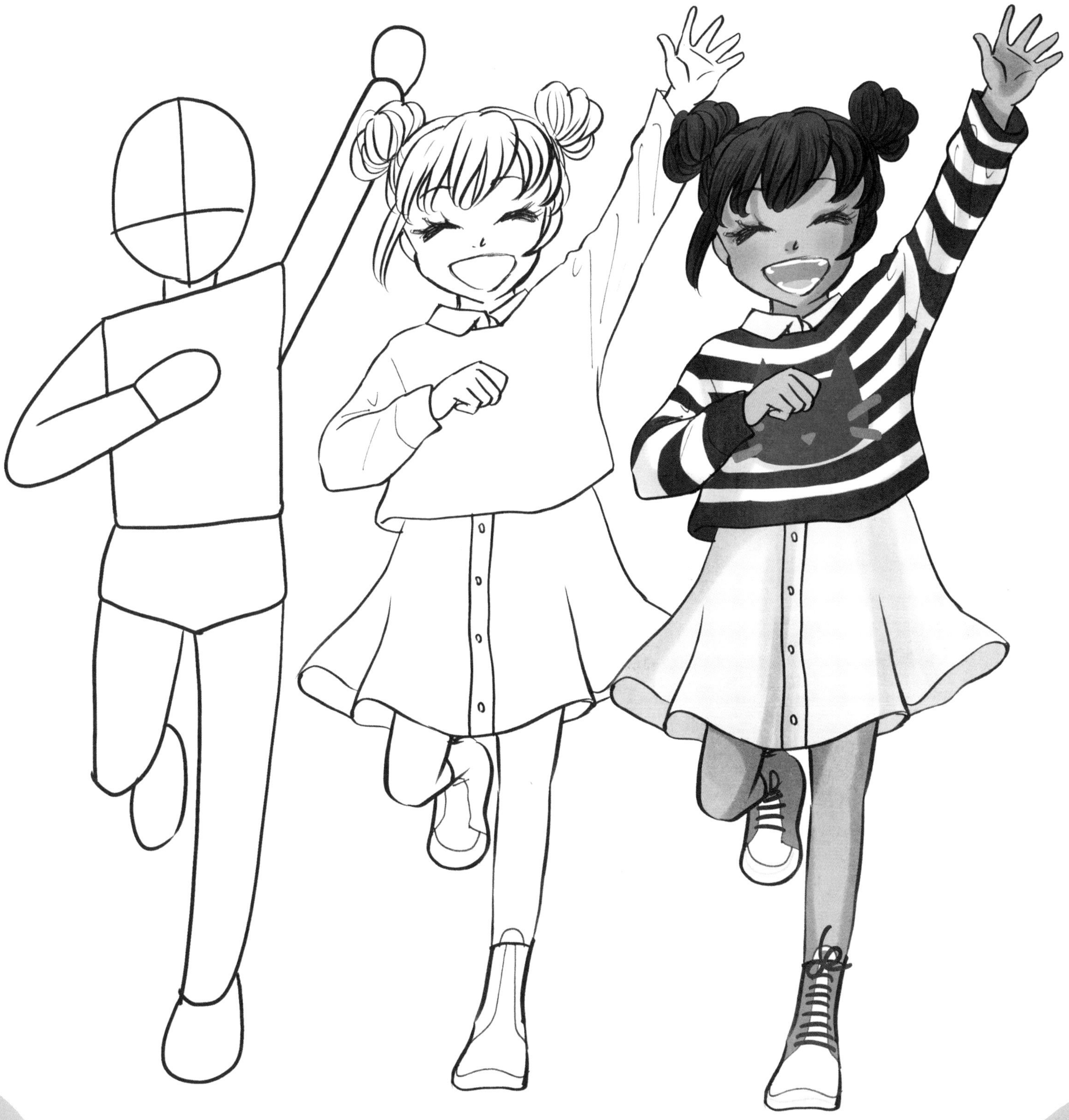

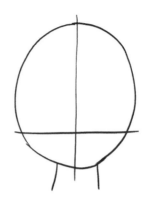

**1** Draw a guideline.

**2** Start drawing her eyes.

**Misako's note:**
Before we start designing manga outfits, let's practice drawing manga faces from various angles! If you would like to draw more kinds of faces, bodies, and hair, check out *How to Draw Kawaii Manga Characters!*

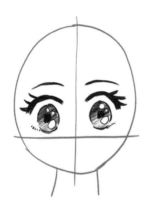

CHIN

**3** Draw bubbles inside her eyes and add colors.

**4** Draw face lines and a guide dot on her chin.

**5** Finish drawing the face line.

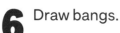

**6** Draw bangs.

**7** Draw detailed hair lines and erase the guidelines to finish.

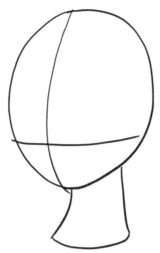

**1** Draw a guideline.

**2** Start drawing her eyes.

**3** Draw bubbles inside her eyes and add colors.

**4** Draw a face line from her cheek.

**5** Dear wavy bangs.

**6** Erase the guidelines to finish.

**1** Draw a guideline.

**2** Start drawing her eyes.

**3** Draw a face from the right side.

**4** Start drawing hair lines to the top.

**5** Draw her headline and the outline of a hair bun.

**6** Draw detailed hair lines.

**7** Erase the guidelines to finish.

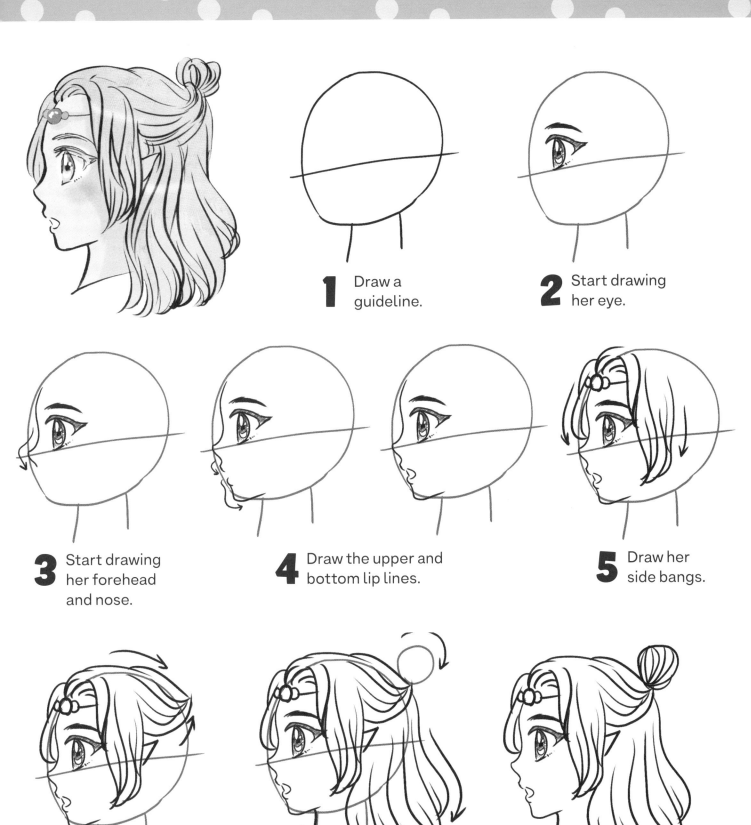

**1** Draw a guideline.

**2** Start drawing her eye.

**3** Start drawing her forehead and nose.

**4** Draw the upper and bottom lip lines.

**5** Draw her side bangs.

**6** Add the rest of her hair.

**7** Erase the guidelines to finish.

# Tween Boy with Spiky Hair

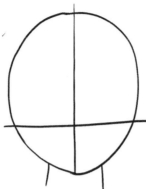

**1** Draw rough guidelines.

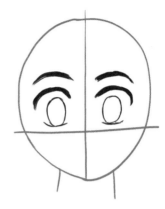

**2** Start drawing his eyebrows and eyes.

**Misako's note:**
I'll show you two faces of tween and teen boys here. Pay attention to the size of their facial features because they're different from girls' features.

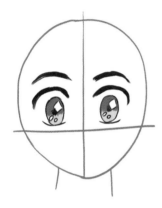

**3** Draw bubbles inside his eyes and add colors.

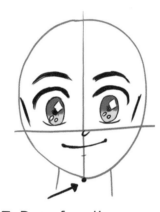

**4** Draw face lines and a guide dot on his chin.

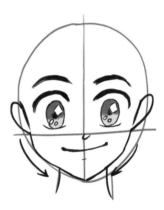

**5** Finish drawing the face lines.

**6** Draw bangs.

**7** Start drawing his spiky hair from the top to the right side. Make sure to draw short spikes under his ear.

**8** Erase the guidelines and add some colors at the end.

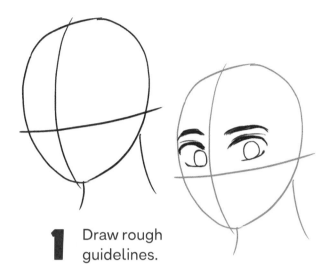

**1** Draw rough guidelines.

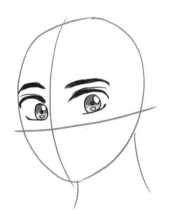

**2** Draw bubbles inside his eyes and add colors.

**3** Draw a face line from his forehead.

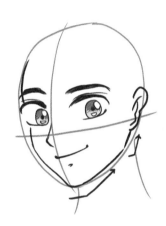

**4** Draw his chin a little bigger and stronger than a girl's.

**5** Draw bangs.

**6** His back hair gets shorter under his ear.

**7** Erase the guidelines and add some colors at the end. You can create shiny spots with an eraser.

# KAWAII SCHOOL OUTFITS

**Misako's note:**
What do you think is the most popular manga outfit to draw? It's a school outfit! You can transform your uniform or everyday clothes into something fun and kawaii!

# Manga School Outfit Examples

I'll show three different outfits here.
A sailor uniform is a must-draw school uniform!
Let's find out which one is your favorite to draw.

スクール

SPORTY
CASUAL

See
page
20!

SAILOR UNIFORM

See
page
16!

HIGH
SCHOOL
UNIFORM
WITH
KNITTED
VEST

See
page
18!

# Sailor Uniform

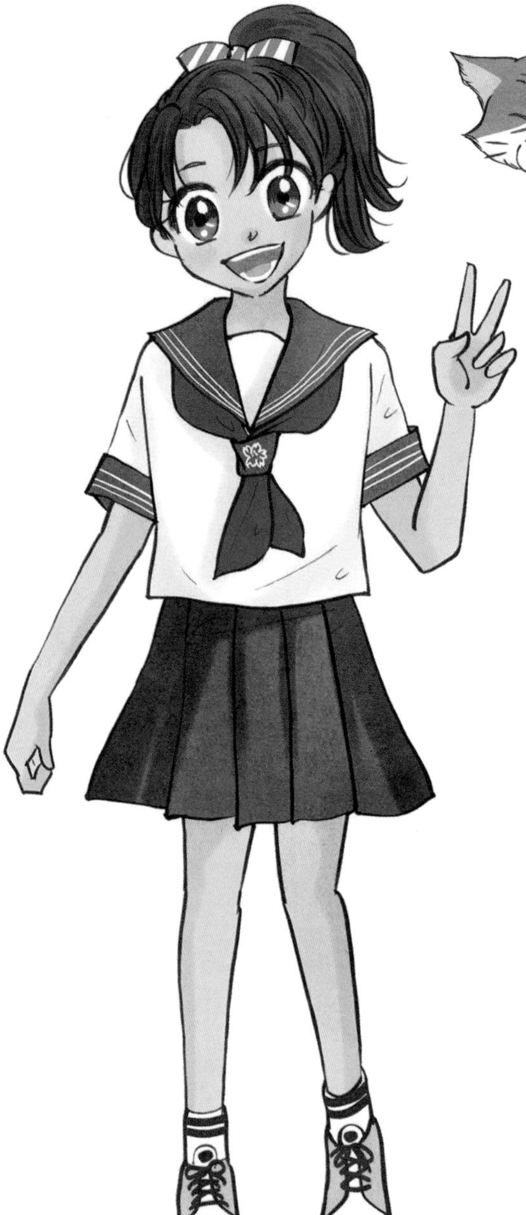

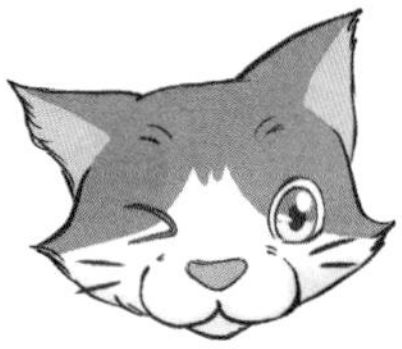

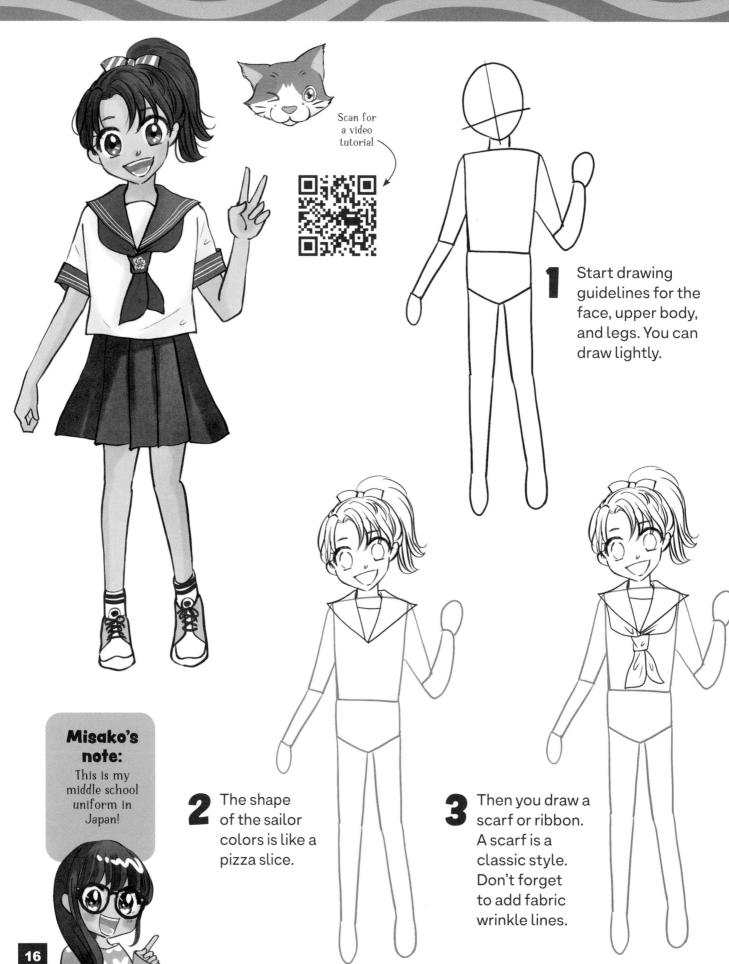

Scan for a video tutorial

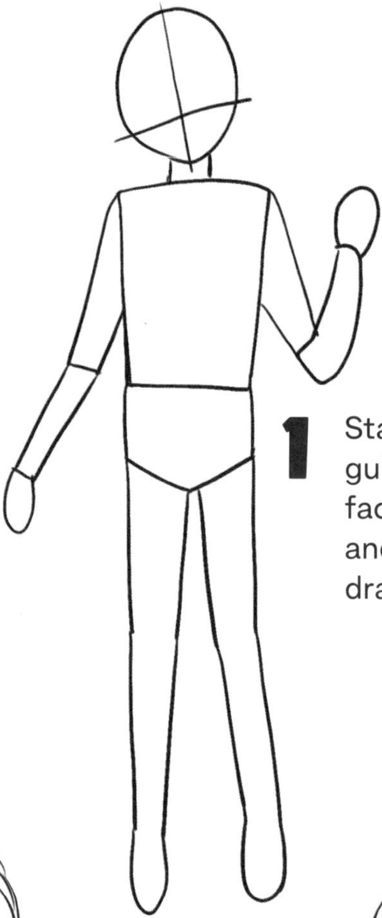

**1** Start drawing guidelines for the face, upper body, and legs. You can draw lightly.

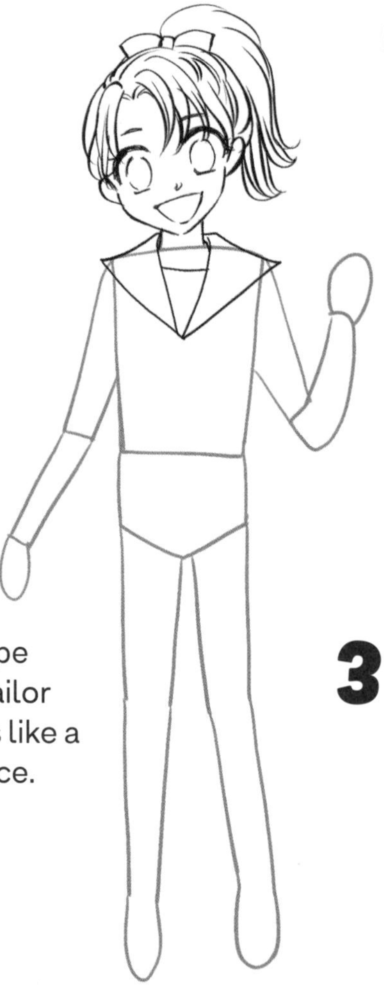

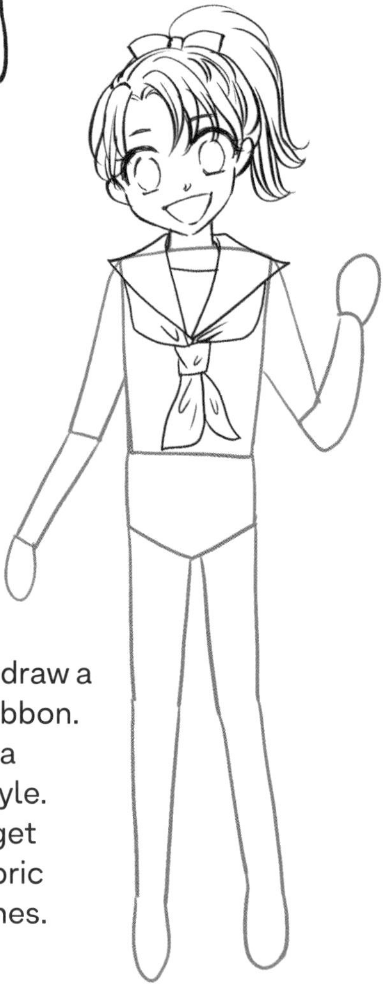

**Misako's note:**

This is my middle school uniform in Japan!

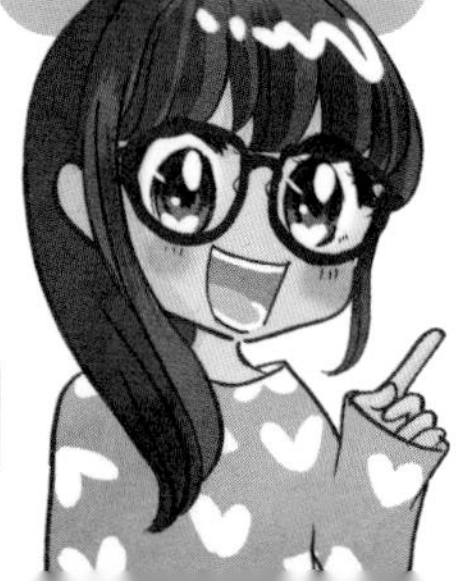

**2** The shape of the sailor colors is like a pizza slice.

**3** Then you draw a scarf or ribbon. A scarf is a classic style. Don't forget to add fabric wrinkle lines.

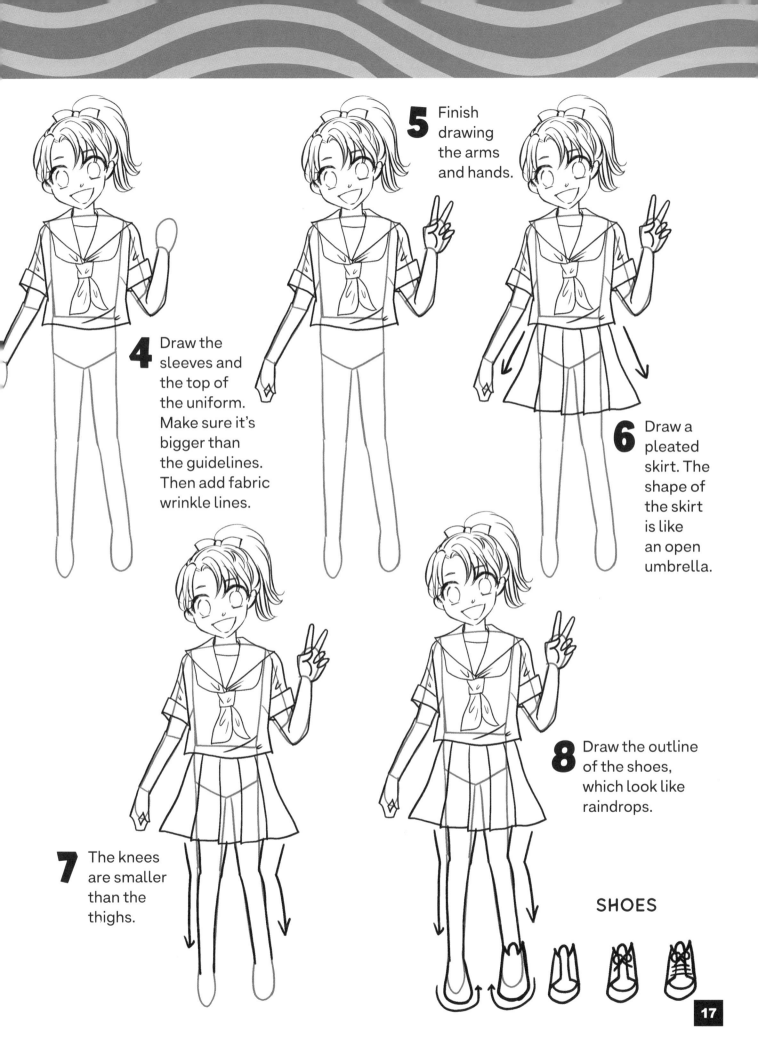

**5** Finish drawing the arms and hands.

**4** Draw the sleeves and the top of the uniform. Make sure it's bigger than the guidelines. Then add fabric wrinkle lines.

**6** Draw a pleated skirt. The shape of the skirt is like an open umbrella.

**7** The knees are smaller than the thighs.

**8** Draw the outline of the shoes, which look like raindrops.

SHOES

# High School Uniform with Knitted Vest

**1** Start with guidelines. Her upper body will be longer than a tween's body.

**2** Draw colors and add fabric wrinkle lines.

**3** Draw strings and a bow underneath the collar. Another option is a tie, which is a cool look.

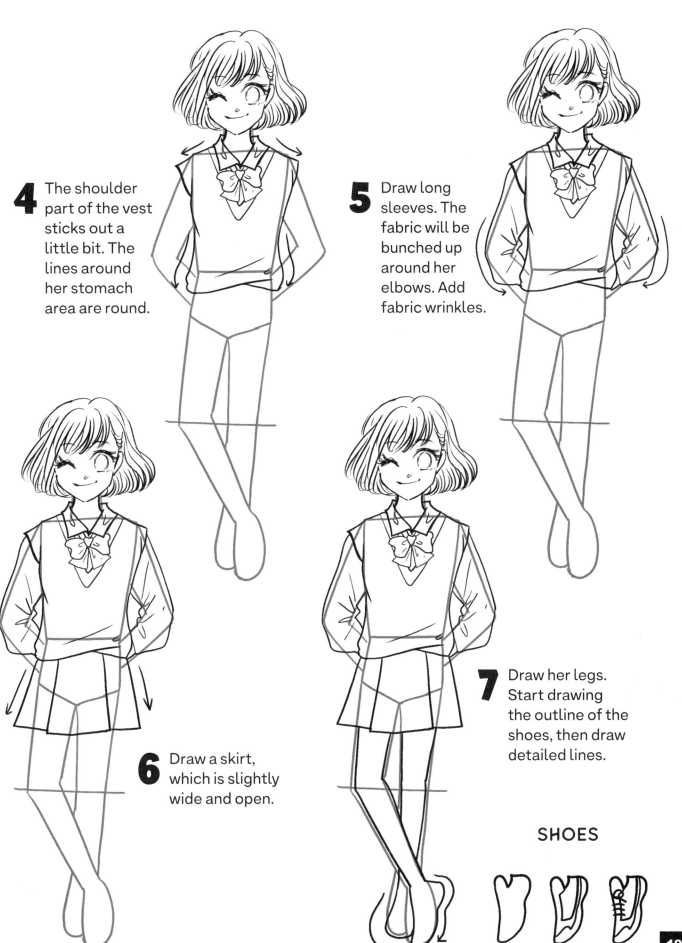

**4** The shoulder part of the vest sticks out a little bit. The lines around her stomach area are round.

**5** Draw long sleeves. The fabric will be bunched up around her elbows. Add fabric wrinkles.

**6** Draw a skirt, which is slightly wide and open.

**7** Draw her legs. Start drawing the outline of the shoes, then draw detailed lines.

**SHOES**

**Misako's note:**
Leggings and an oversized hoodie with a Harajuku logo are must-have items! An oversized outfit is very useful and kawaii to draw! You can add any logos or kawaii graphics to make a one-of-kind hoodie!

原宿♥

**1** Draw guidelines. Her left hand is holding a backpack.

**2** Draw a hoodie, which wraps her neck. Add strings.

**3** Draw a long sleeve and top. Make sure the shape around the wrist and waist is round.

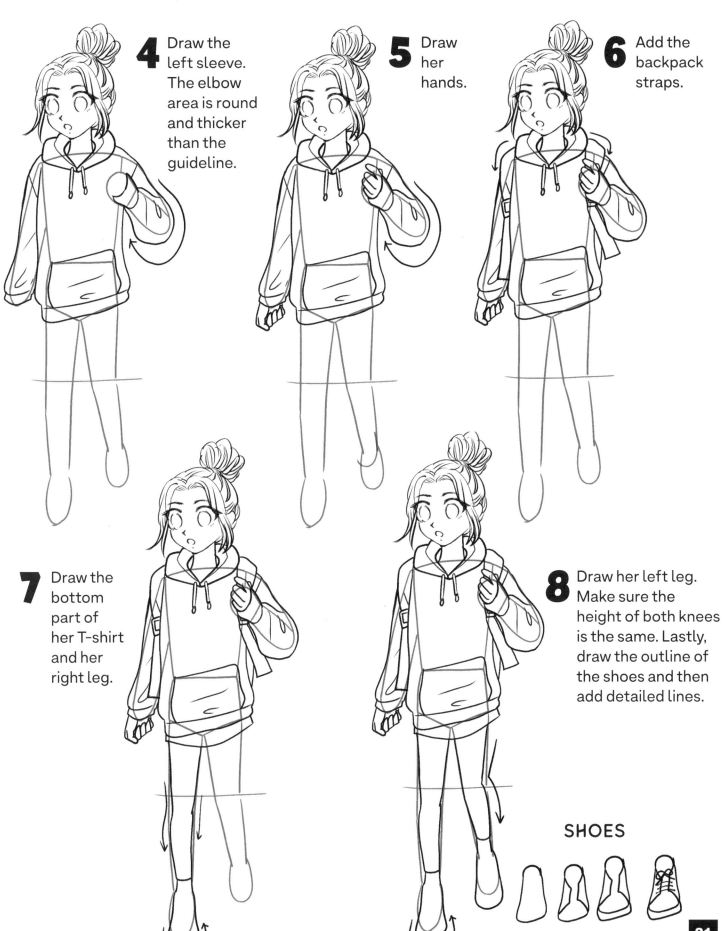

**4** Draw the left sleeve. The elbow area is round and thicker than the guideline.

**5** Draw her hands.

**6** Add the backpack straps.

**7** Draw the bottom part of her T-shirt and her right leg.

**8** Draw her left leg. Make sure the height of both knees is the same. Lastly, draw the outline of the shoes and then add detailed lines.

SHOES

# SCHOOL OUTFITS INSPIRATIONS

**PREPPY SCHOOL UNIFORM WITH JACKET**

See page 26!

**TWEEN BOY IN A SPORTY OUTFIT**

See page 24!

**Misako's note:**
When you draw a sweater, blouse, or skirt, don't forget to add fabric wrinkles.

**SHIRT AND DRESS OUTFIT**

See page 30!

**TEEN BOY IN A SCHOOL UNIFORM**

See page 28!

**Misako's note:**
An oversized jacket or shirt works great for these casual outfits. Add some patterns and logos to make them extra kawaii!

# Tween Boy in a Sporty Outfit

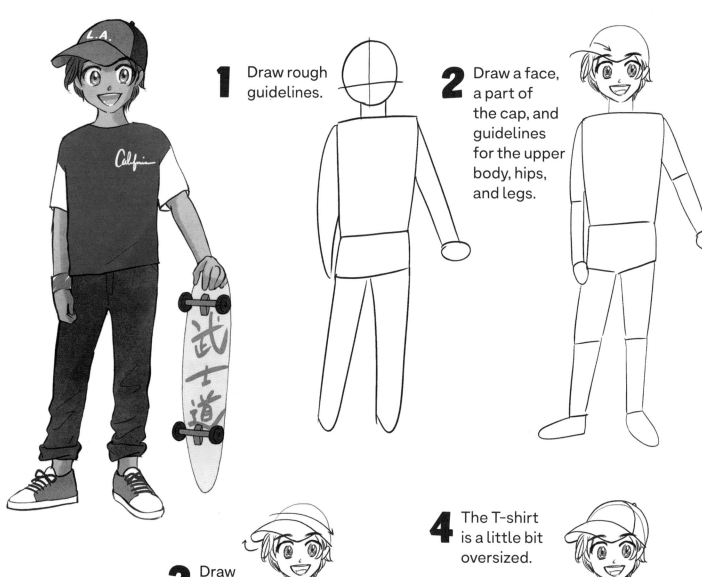

**1** Draw rough guidelines.

**2** Draw a face, a part of the cap, and guidelines for the upper body, hips, and legs.

**3** Draw the rim of the cap.

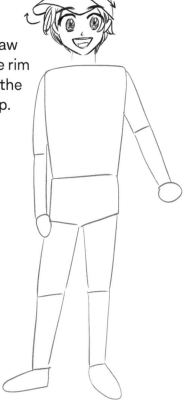

**4** The T-shirt is a little bit oversized.

**Misako's note:**
You don't want to draw too tall or wide here. His body size is very similar to a tween girl's but slightly different. The key will be baggy and casual clothes.

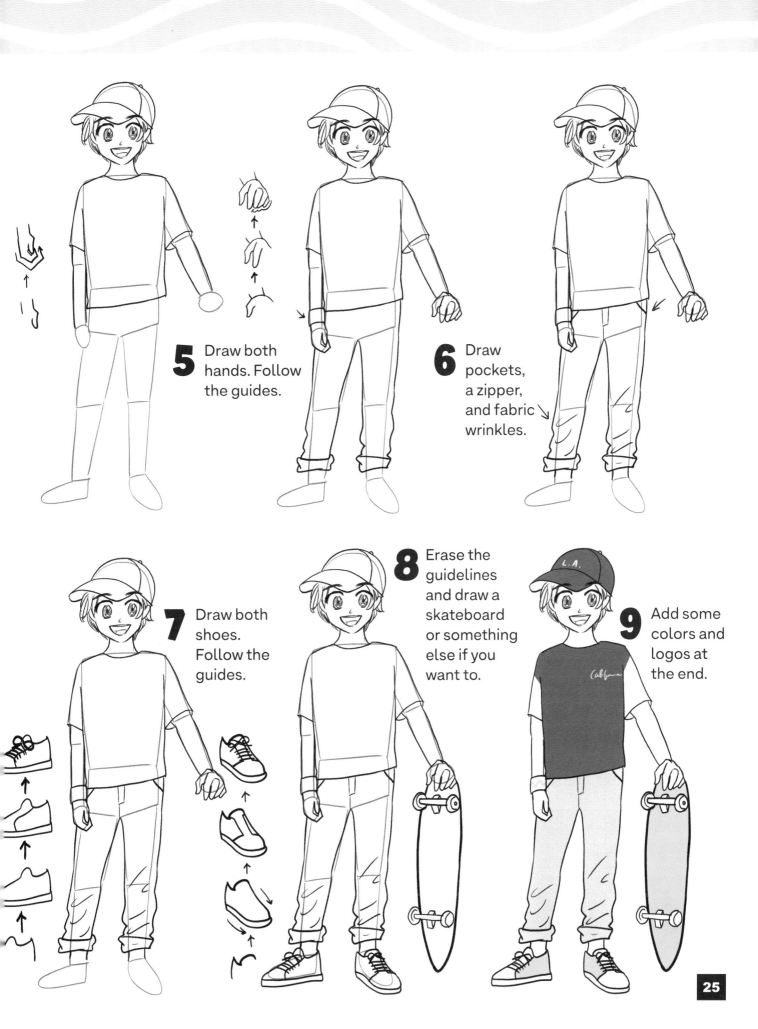

**5** Draw both hands. Follow the guides.

**6** Draw pockets, a zipper, and fabric wrinkles.

**7** Draw both shoes. Follow the guides.

**8** Erase the guidelines and draw a skateboard or something else if you want to.

**9** Add some colors and logos at the end.

# Preppy School Uniform with Jacket

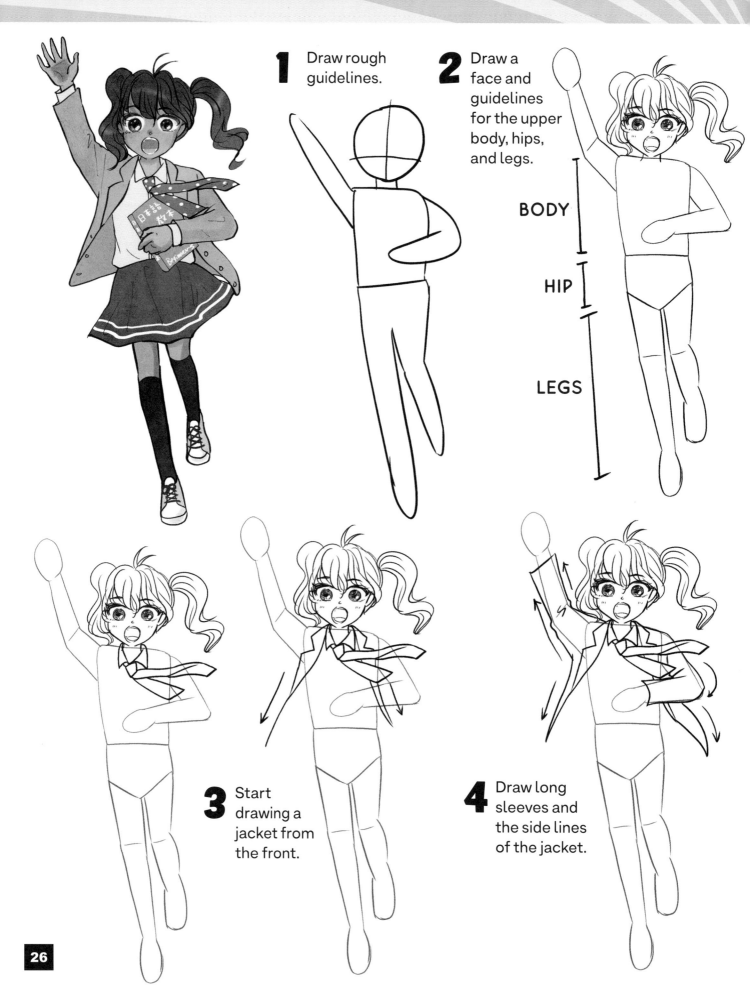

**1** Draw rough guidelines.

**2** Draw a face and guidelines for the upper body, hips, and legs.

BODY

HIP

LEGS

**3** Start drawing a jacket from the front.

**4** Draw long sleeves and the side lines of the jacket.

**5** Draw both hands. Follow the guides.

**6** Draw both shoes. Follow the guides.

**7** Erase the guidelines and add some colors at the end.

**Misako's note:**

This is a great outfit for fall and winter. You see this in Japan a lot! You can add a knitted sweater underneath if you want.

**1** Draw rough guidelines.

**2** Draw a face and guidelines for the upper body, hips, and legs.

**3** Draw the front part of his jacket.

Scan for a video tutorial →

**Misako's note:**
This is a classic and useful outfit for manga teen boys. I can't wait to show you how to draw this!

**4** Draw sleeves and his left hand. Follow the guide.

**5** Draw a tie, a line in the center, and a pocket.

**6** Draw his sneakers. Follow the guides.

**7** Erase the guidelines and draw fabric wrinkles.

**8** Add some colors and patterns to the tie at the end.

**1** Draw rough guidelines.

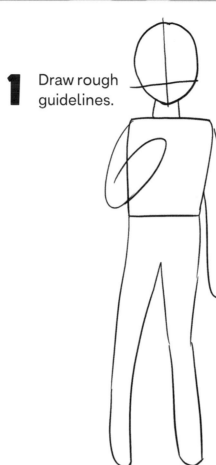

**2** Draw a face and guidelines for the upper body, hips, and legs.

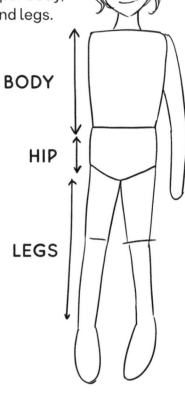

BODY

HIP

LEGS

**3** Draw fabric wrinkles inside the shirt.

### Misako's note:

An oversized shirt is great outwear for all seasons. Add patterns to the shirt if you want.

**4** Draw both hands. Follow the guides.

**5** Draw a book.

**6** Draw her right shoe. Follow the guide.

**7** Draw her left shoe. Follow the guide.

**8** Erase the guidelines and add some colors at the end.

31

# SCHOOL ACCESSORIES INSPIRATIONS

PENCIL CASE

WRITING TOOLS

SCRUNCHIE

SCHOOL BUS

WATCH

TAPE

CLIPS

NOTEBOOK

LUNCH BAG

BENTO BOX

WATER BOTTLE

APPLE

## BACKPACK

## SNEAKERS

### Misako's note:
You can add keychains, pins, and more to these samples. Customize them as much as you want!

Draw Manga with Misako!

Misako's note:
Check out what she's saying and then draw her body!

You can print out more copies to draw with me here!

I drew her face.
Now you draw her body and outfit.

"Today is the first day at school! I love my school uniform, especially this kawaii bow!"

**I drew her face.**
**Now you draw her body and outfit.**

## Draw Manga with Misako!

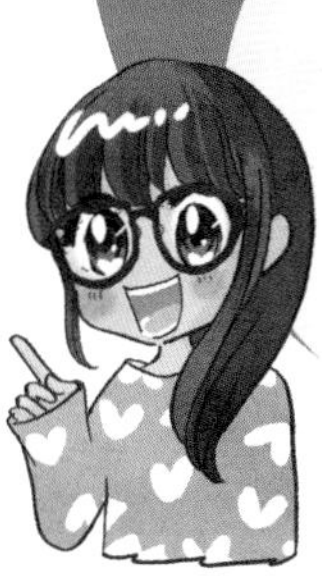

**Misako's note:**
Check out what she's saying and then draw her body!

You can print out more copies to draw with me here!

"It's lunchtime!
I have my bento box
and lunch bag!"

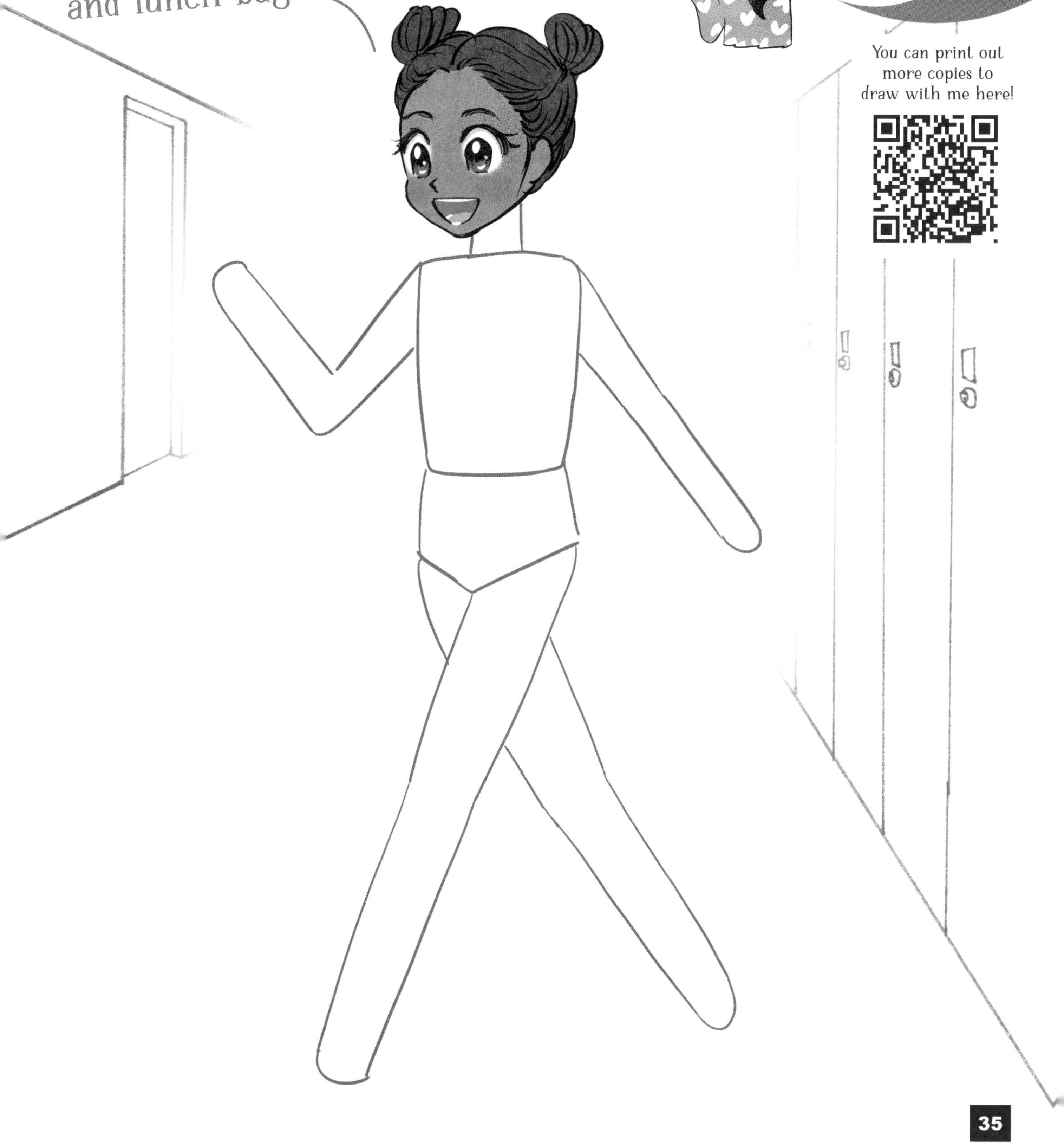

# KAWAII FANTASY OUTFITS

### Misako's note:
Who doesn't like to design outfits for fantasy characters? Use your imagination and follow your heart. Don't hold back! I enjoy drawing flowy dresses and wings for fairies. What about you?

# Fantasy Outfit Examples

These three outfits are great examples of fantasy outfits. Use the entire page to draw the character but leave space for various accessories. Don't be shy about drawing their dresses big and fluffy! Bigger is better here.

**PRINCESS**

See page 42!

**WITCH**

See page 40!

**FAIRY**

See page 38!

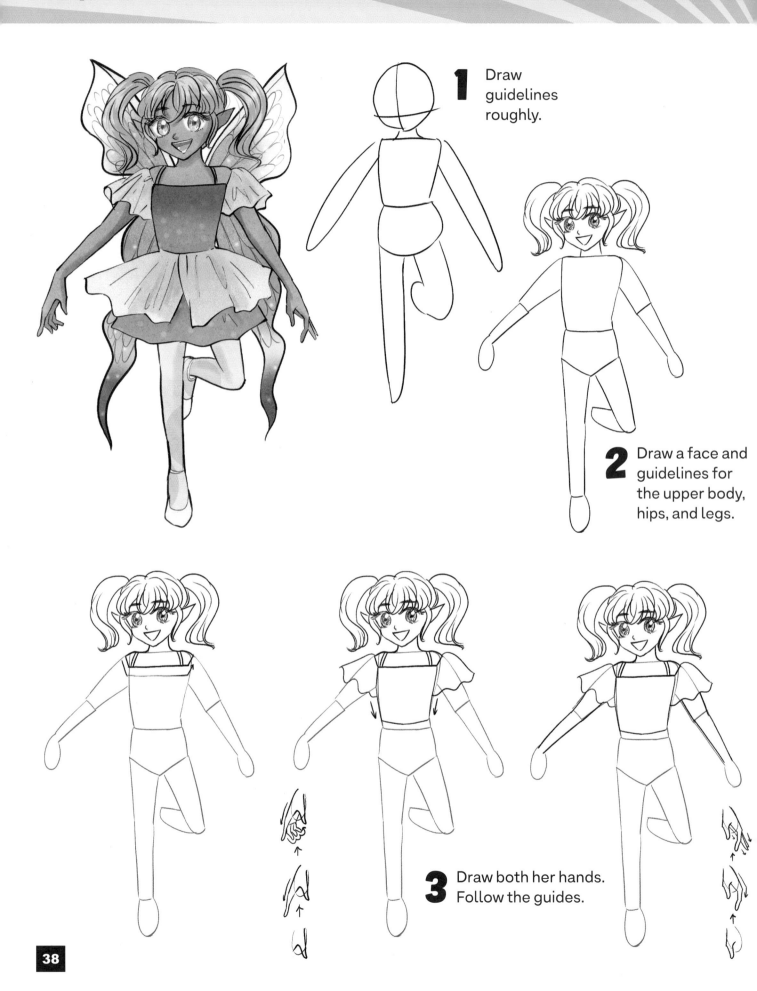

**1** Draw guidelines roughly.

**2** Draw a face and guidelines for the upper body, hips, and legs.

**3** Draw both her hands. Follow the guides.

**4** Add a top with ruffled short sleeves and a layered skirt. Then draw her legs and add slippers.

**5** After you finish drawing her outfit, draw guidelines for the wings.

**6** Draw wavy wings.

**7** Draw patterns inside.

**8** Erase the guidelines and add some patterns at the end.

**Misako's note:**

Pay attention to the design of her wings in addition to her outfit. Let's create a beautiful outfit from head to toe!

**1** Draw rough guidelines.

**2** Draw a face and guidelines for the upper body, hips, and legs.

**3** Draw a cape with fabric wrinkles in it. Finish the arms.

**4** Draw both hands. Follow the guides.

**5** Draw a top, a layered skirt, fabric wrinkles, and legs.

**6** Draw both shoes. Follow the guides.

**7** Draw a broom.

**8** Draw a cat. I show detailed guides on page 51.

**9** Erase the guidelines and add some colors at the end.

**1** Draw rough guidelines.

**2** Draw a face and guidelines for the upper body and skirt.

**3** Draw fabric wrinkles inside the frills.

**4** Draw a bow and the letter "x" in the center of the upper body.

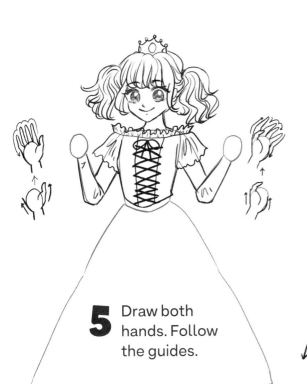

**5** Draw both hands. Follow the guides.

**6** Draw a lot of fabric wrinkles inside her dress.

**7** Draw roses. Follow the guides. Erase the guidelines and add some colors at the end.

# FANTASY OUTFITS INSPIRATIONS

ELF

VAMPIRE

See page 46!

Scan for a video tutorial →

**Misako's note:**
Drawing layered clothes like above will be the key to creating kawaii and whimsical fantasy characters.

Scan for a video tutorial

FOX

WARRIOR

See page 48!

**Misako's note:**

First, pick a theme and draw a casual outfit. Then you can design a jacket, coat, and accessories for their outfit!

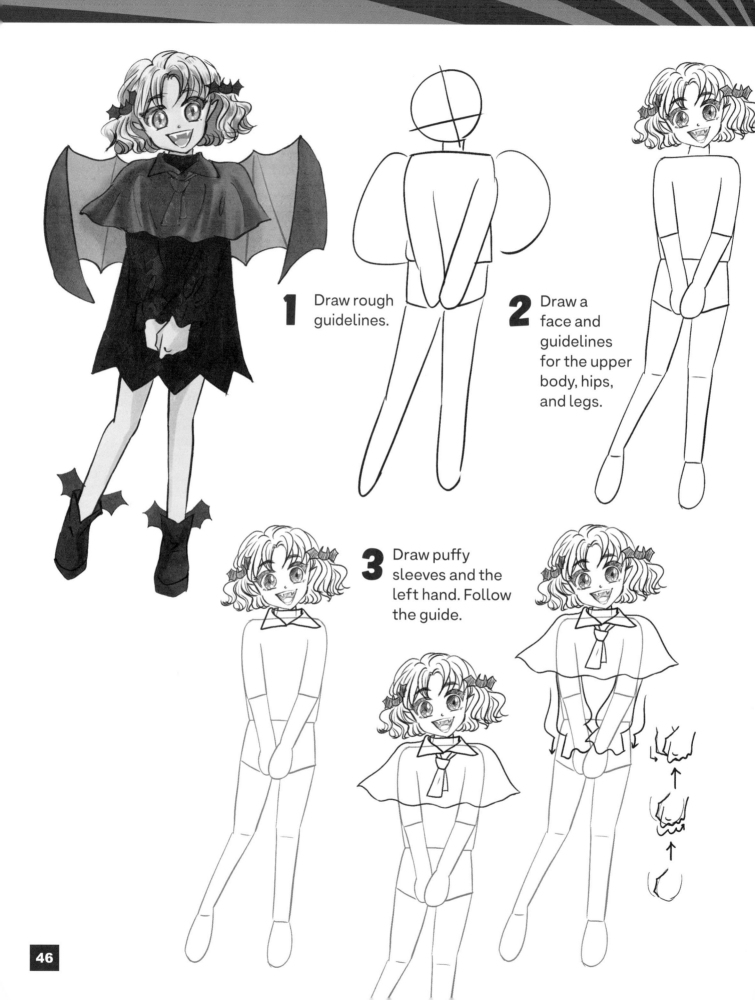

**1** Draw rough guidelines.

**2** Draw a face and guidelines for the upper body, hips, and legs.

**3** Draw puffy sleeves and the left hand. Follow the guide.

**4** Draw both shoes. Follow the guides.

**5** Start drawing wings, which look like a bat's.

**6** Erase the guidelines and add some colors at the end.

**Misako's note:**
If you like mysterious and cool characters, a vampire is the best one for you to design. A classic style is a long cape. I made it shorter here to look kawaii and modern. What do you think?

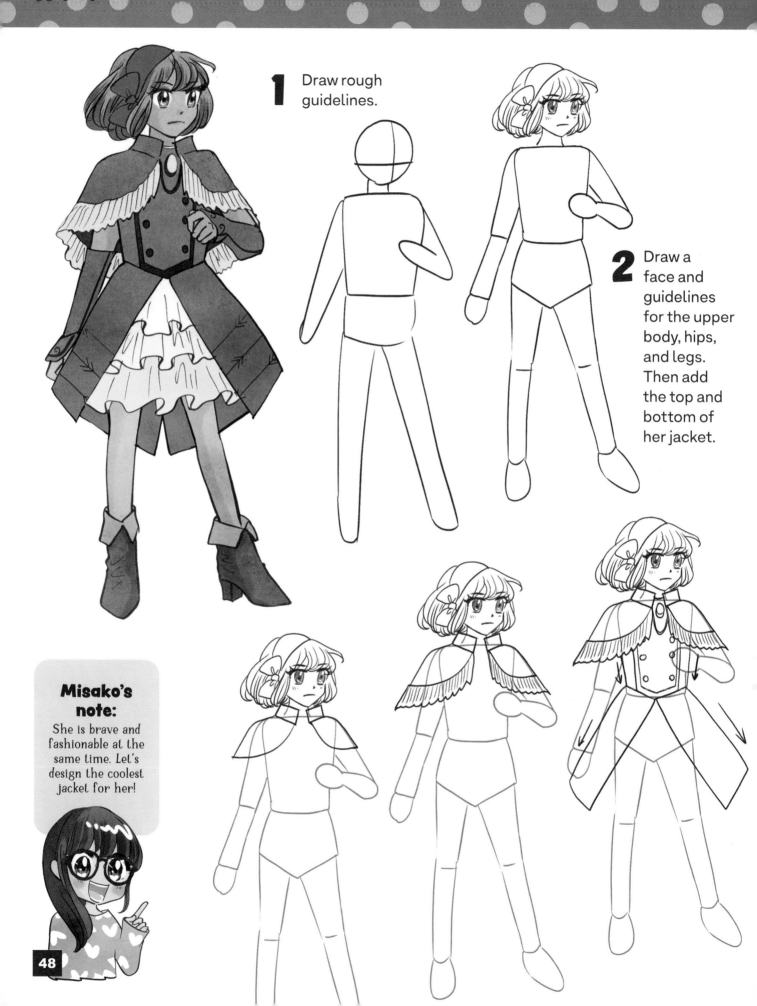

**1** Draw rough guidelines.

**2** Draw a face and guidelines for the upper body, hips, and legs. Then add the top and bottom of her jacket.

### Misako's note:

She is brave and fashionable at the same time. Let's design the coolest jacket for her!

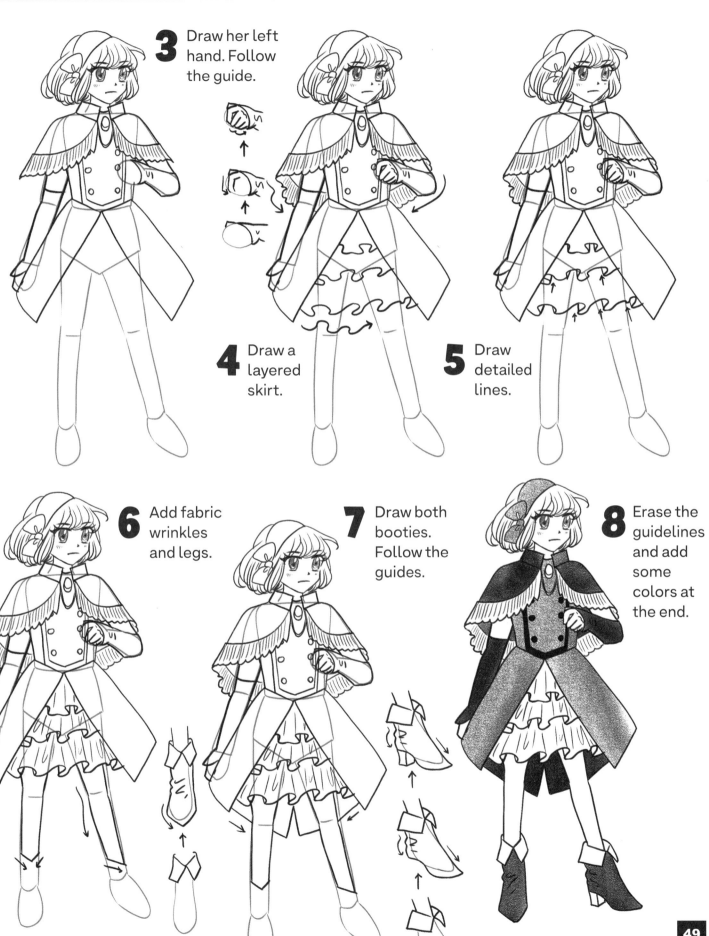

**3** Draw her left hand. Follow the guide.

**4** Draw a layered skirt.

**5** Draw detailed lines.

**6** Add fabric wrinkles and legs.

**7** Draw both booties. Follow the guides.

**8** Erase the guidelines and add some colors at the end.

# FANTASY ACCESSORIES INSPIRATIONS

NECKLACE

OVERSIZED BOW

TIARA

WINGS

LANTERN

WAND

BOOTIES

FEATHER PEN

ANIMAL EARS

ANIMAL TAIL

# CAT

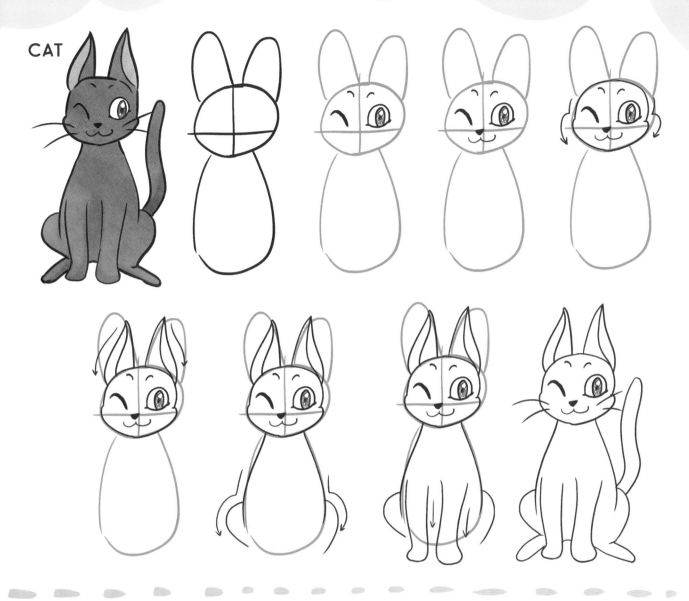

# HAT

**Misako's note:**
You can add more accessories and patterns to these ideas!

# Draw Manga with Misako!

**Misako's note:**
Check out what she's saying and then draw her body!

You can print out more copies to draw with me here!

## I drew her face. Now you draw her body and outfit.

*"I'm a spring fairy. I love flying through beautiful trees and flowers."*

**I drew the guideline.
Now you draw her face and outfit.**

"I'm a student at a witch school.
Look at my cape! Isn't it beautiful?"

# KAWAII HARAJUKU OUTFITS

**Misako's note:**
Harajuku fashion is full of kawaii-ness! I used to dress up and hang out in Harajuku with my friends. This fashion is the symbol of kawaii culture. I'll help you design your original Harajuku outfits!

# Harajuku Kawaii Outfit Examples

DECORA

See page 56!

KAWAII DOLL

STREET ROCK

See page 58!

**Misako's note:**

I'd like you to design colorful and fun outfits here. These three types are always trendy and popular! Which style do you like to design or wear? Let's pick one and start drawing!

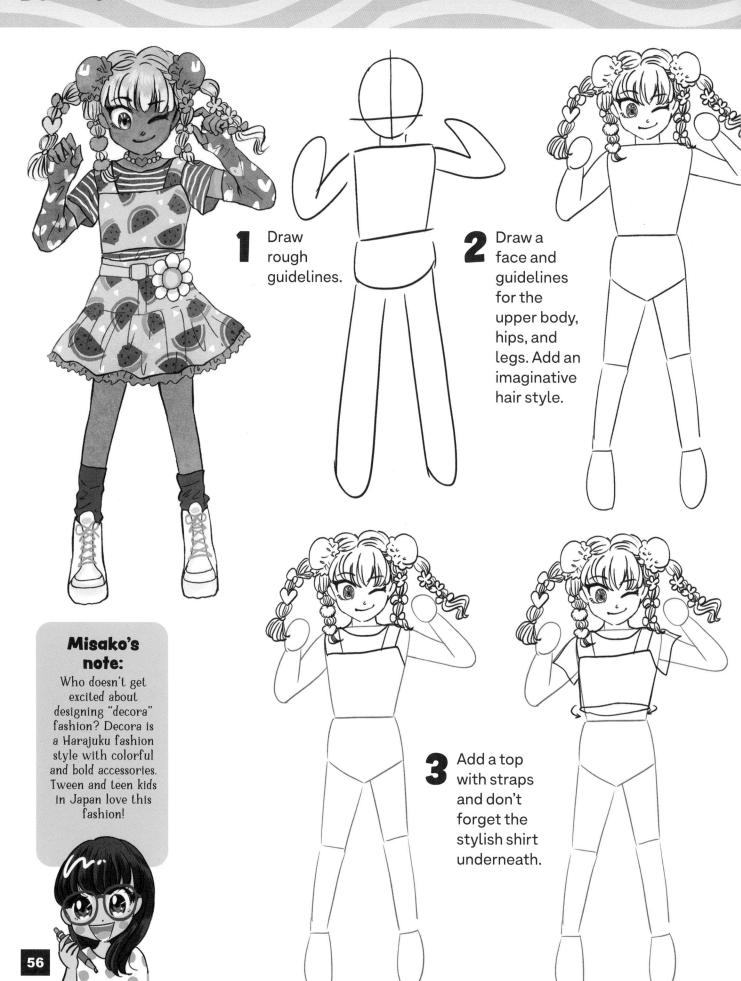

**1** Draw rough guidelines.

**2** Draw a face and guidelines for the upper body, hips, and legs. Add an imaginative hair style.

**3** Add a top with straps and don't forget the stylish shirt underneath.

### Misako's note:
Who doesn't get excited about designing "decora" fashion? Decora is a Harajuku fashion style with colorful and bold accessories. Tween and teen kids in Japan love this fashion!

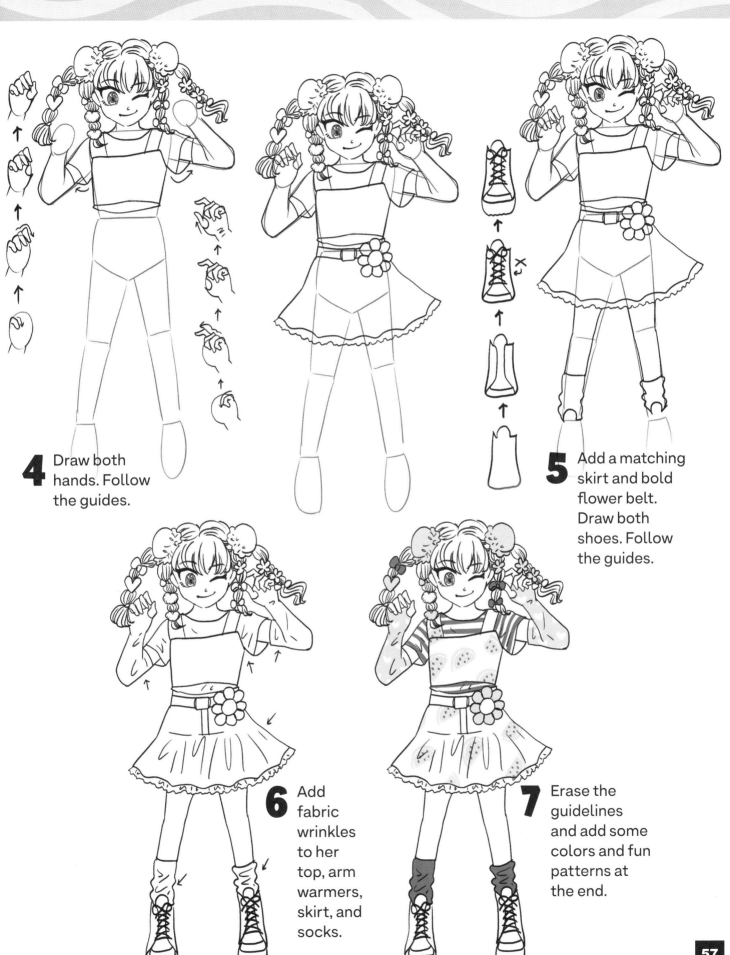

**4** Draw both hands. Follow the guides.

**5** Add a matching skirt and bold flower belt. Draw both shoes. Follow the guides.

**6** Add fabric wrinkles to her top, arm warmers, skirt, and socks.

**7** Erase the guidelines and add some colors and fun patterns at the end.

**1** Draw rough guidelines.

**2** Draw a face and guidelines for the upper body, hips, and legs.

**3** Start drawing the hoodie.

**4** Draw the wrists fluffy and puffy. Oversized is the key here!

**5** Draw her left hand. Follow the guide.

**Misako's note:**
This style is a bit more casual and an everyday outfit, which is useful. I want you to add tons of kawaii accessories to make it Harajuku style!

猫サマ!

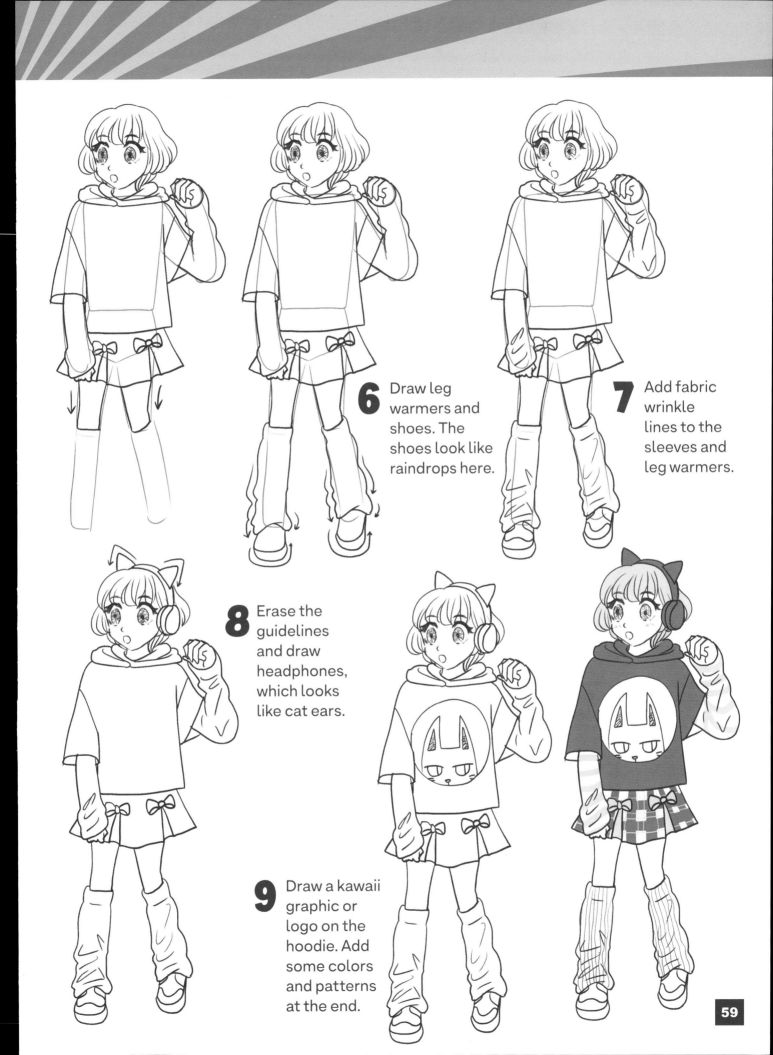

**6** Draw leg warmers and shoes. The shoes look like raindrops here.

**7** Add fabric wrinkle lines to the sleeves and leg warmers.

**8** Erase the guidelines and draw headphones, which looks like cat ears.

**9** Draw a kawaii graphic or logo on the hoodie. Add some colors and patterns at the end.

# HARAJUKU OUTFITS INSPIRATIONS

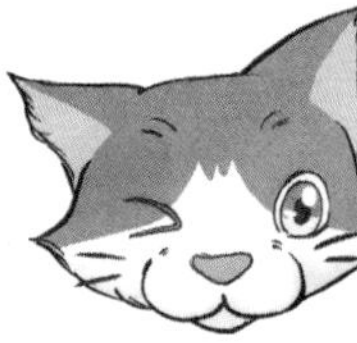

Scan for a video tutorial

COOL GOTHIC

See page 62!

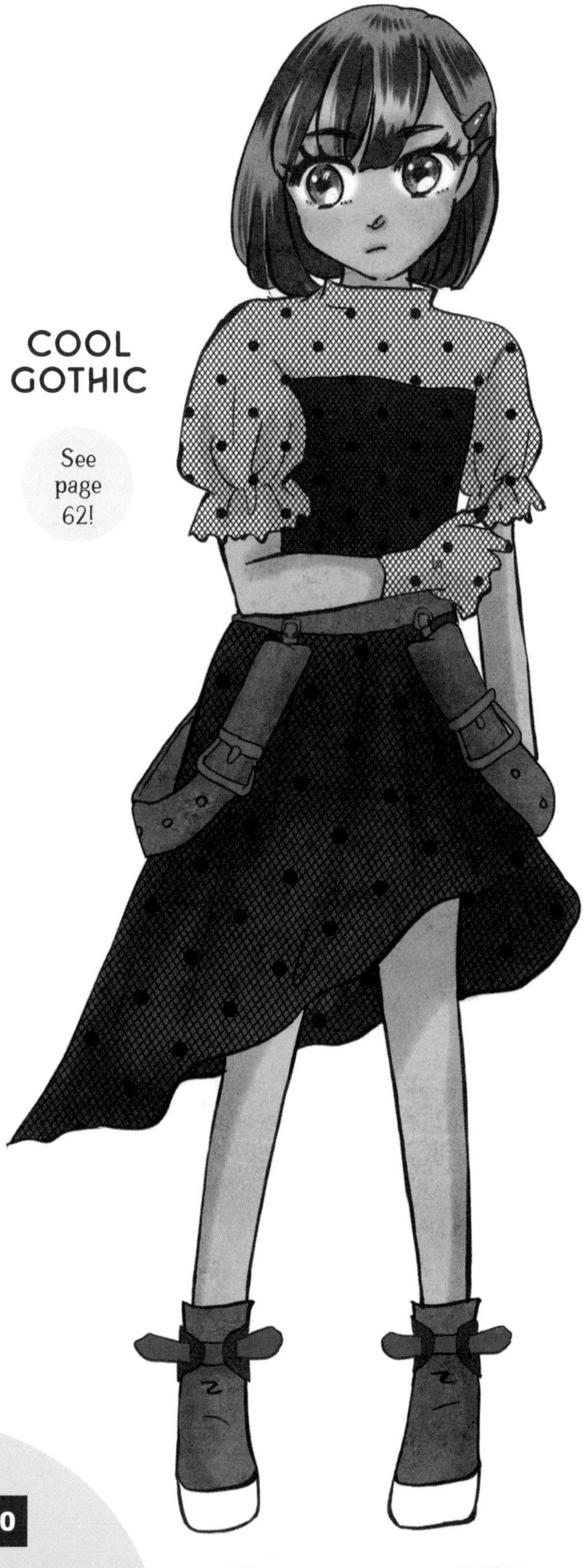

YUME (DREAM) KAWAII

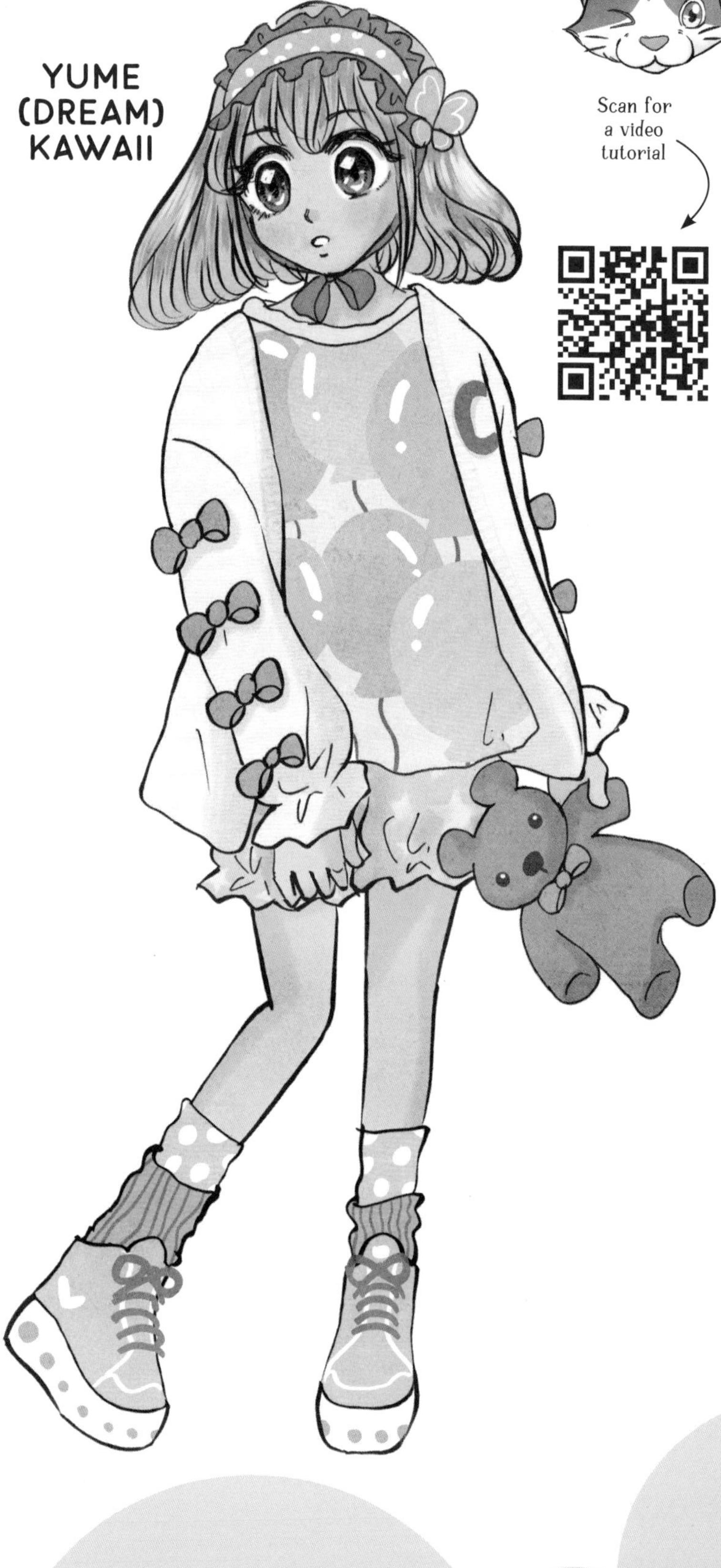

**ARTY AND TOMBOY**

**ANIMAL KAWAII**

See page 64!

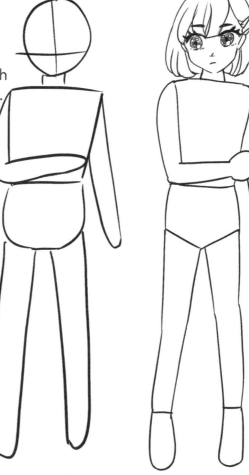

**1** Draw rough guidelines.

**2** Draw a face and guidelines for the upper body, hips, and legs.

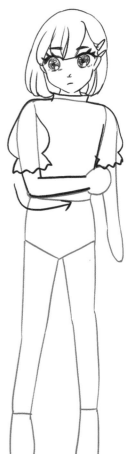

**3** Draw puffy sleeves and her right hand. Follow the guide.

### Misako's note:
If you like a style that is a little more mature and cool, this is a perfect one to draw!

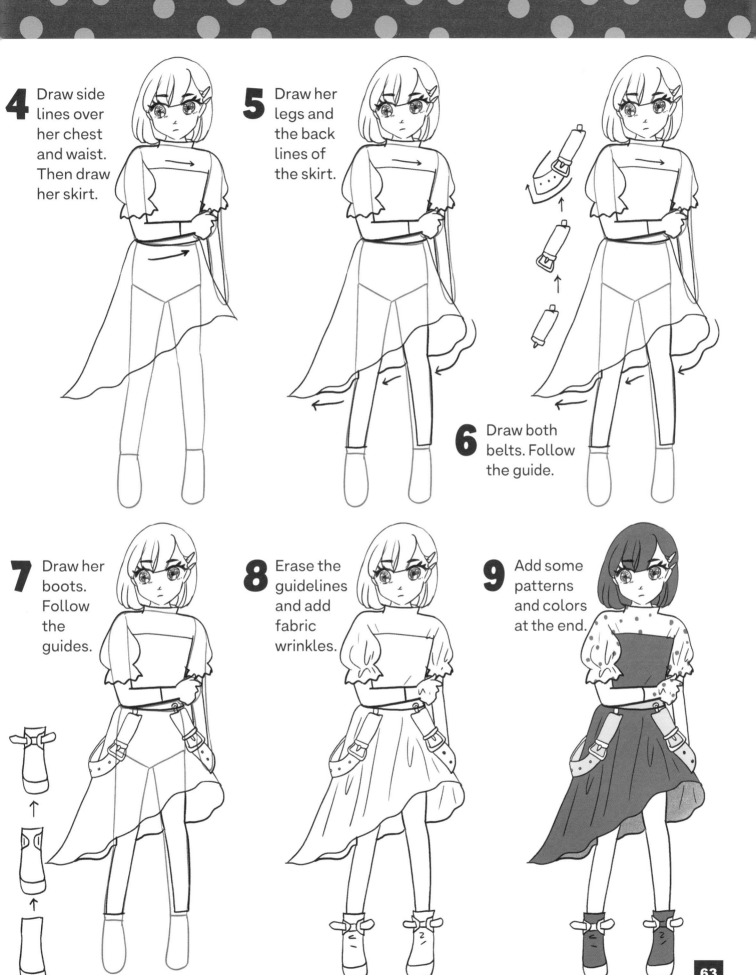

**4** Draw side lines over her chest and waist. Then draw her skirt.

**5** Draw her legs and the back lines of the skirt.

**6** Draw both belts. Follow the guide.

**7** Draw her boots. Follow the guides.

**8** Erase the guidelines and add fabric wrinkles.

**9** Add some patterns and colors at the end.

**1** Draw rough guidelines.

**2** Draw a face and guidelines for the upper body, hips, and legs.

**3** Draw a hoodie, bangs, and her side hair first.

**4** Draw the rest of her hair and neck lines.

**5** Draw both hands. Follow the guides.

**6** Draw leg warmers wider than her legs and fluffy.

**7** Erase the guidelines and add some patterns at the end.

ウサギ

Bunny

## Draw Manga with Misako!

**Misako's note:**

Check out what she's saying and then draw her body!

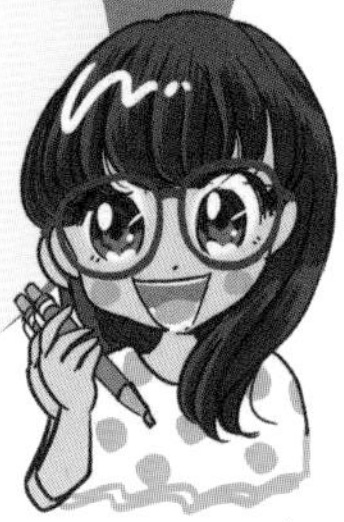

You can print out more copies to draw with me here!

# I drew her face.
# Now you draw her body and outfit.

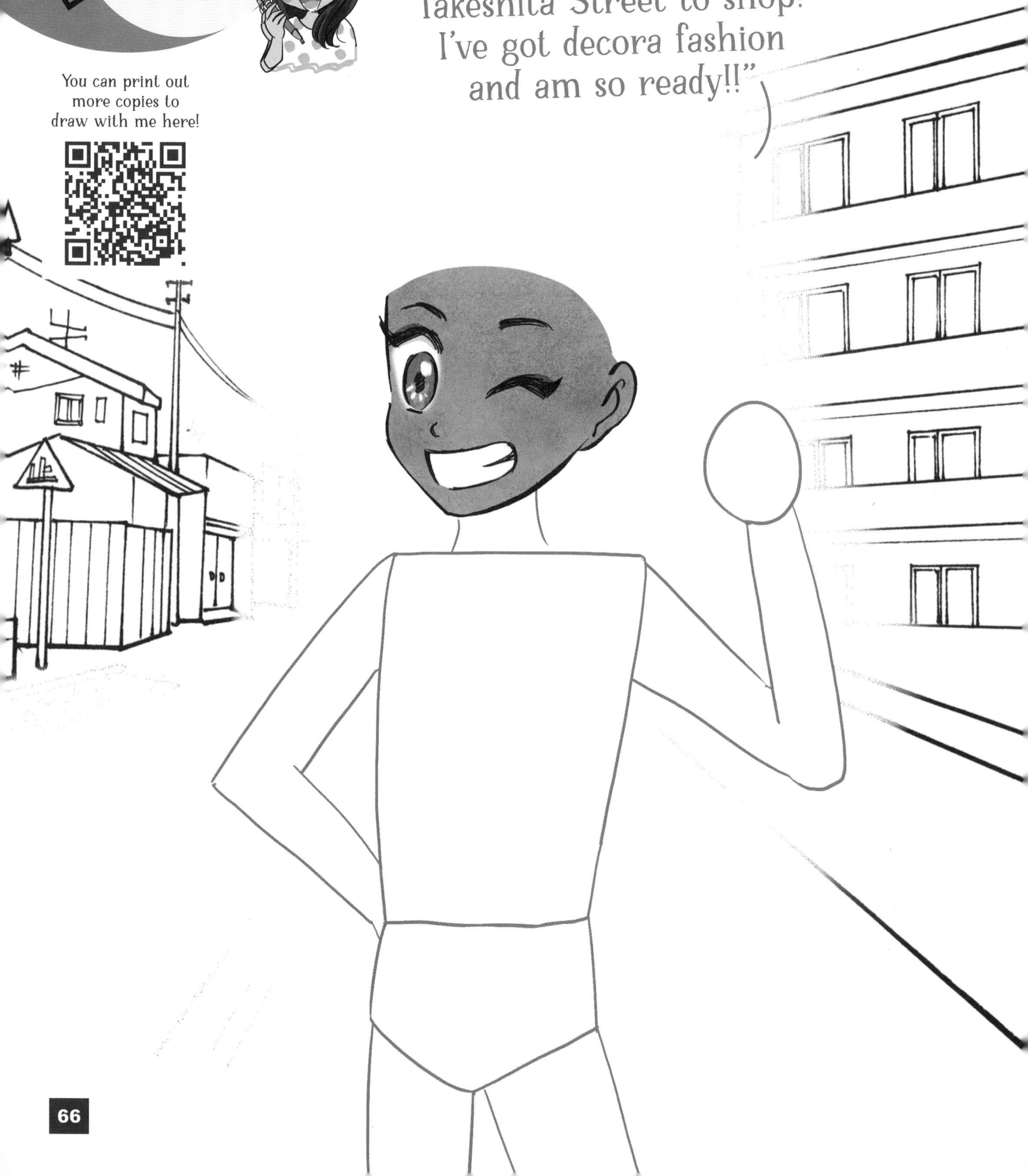
"I'm excited to go to Takeshita Street to shop! I've got decora fashion and am so ready!!"

# I drew guidelines.
# Now you draw her body and outfit.

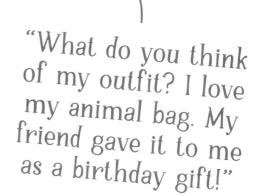

"What do you think of my outfit? I love my animal bag. My friend gave it to me as a birthday gift!"

# KAWAII OUTFITS FOR EVERY SEASON

SUMMER

See page 72!

SPRING

See page 70!

**Misako's note:**
You can pick color themes depending on the season. You can use cherry blossoms for spring and a two-piece breezy dress for summer!

**FALL**

See page 74!

**WINTER**

See page 76!

**Misako's note:**
You can draw layered outfits for fall and elegant holiday dresses for winter! I love designing holiday outfits. Winter is definitely a great theme for manga fashion.

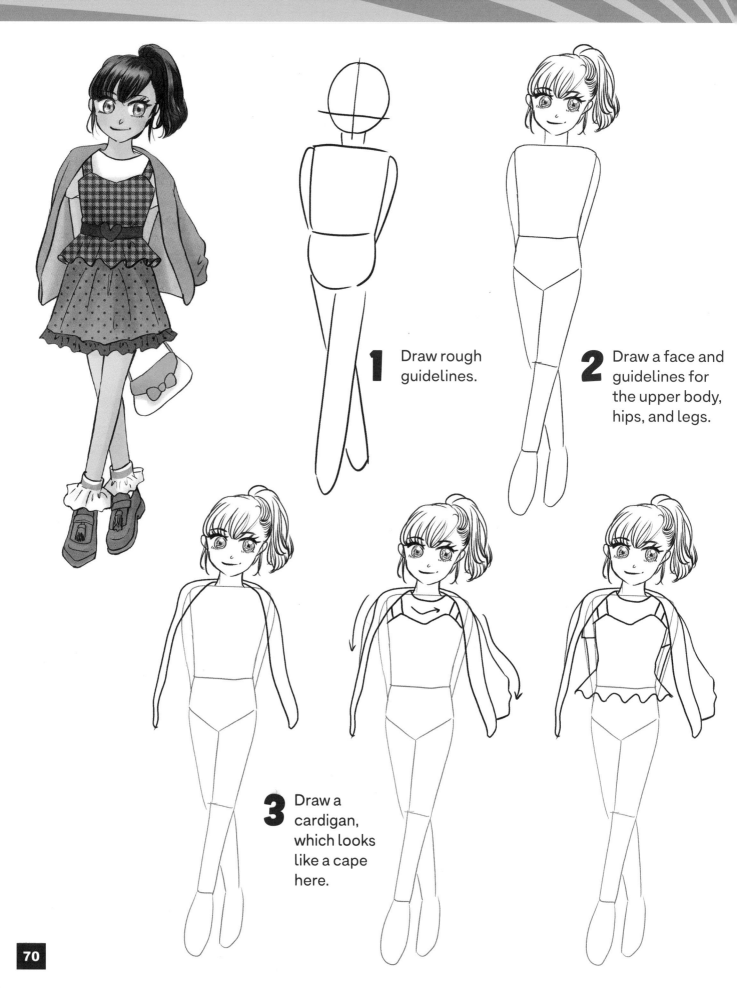

**1** Draw rough guidelines.

**2** Draw a face and guidelines for the upper body, hips, and legs.

**3** Draw a cardigan, which looks like a cape here.

**6** Draw legs and shoes.
Follow the guides.

**4** Don't forget to draw the back lines of the cardigan.

**5** Draw fabric wrinkles around her skirt's waist.

**7** Erase the guidelines and draw a bag.

**8** Add some colors and patterns at the end.

## Misako's note:

A light jacket or cardigan and dress will suit this season. Bring pastel-colored pencils. You'll need them!

**1** Draw rough guidelines.

**2** Draw a face and guidelines for the upper body, hips, and legs.

**3** Draw the back neck lines.

**4** Don't worry about the arms yet. Draw her top and stomach.

**5** Draw her arms and hands. Follow the guides.

**6** Draw her legs and sandals. Follow the guides.

**Misako's note:**
Think about a fun and energetic pose here! Blue sky and sun make her extra happy.

**7** Draw a bow on her back and fabric wrinkles around the skirt.

**8** Erase the guidelines and add some colors at the end.

# Fall

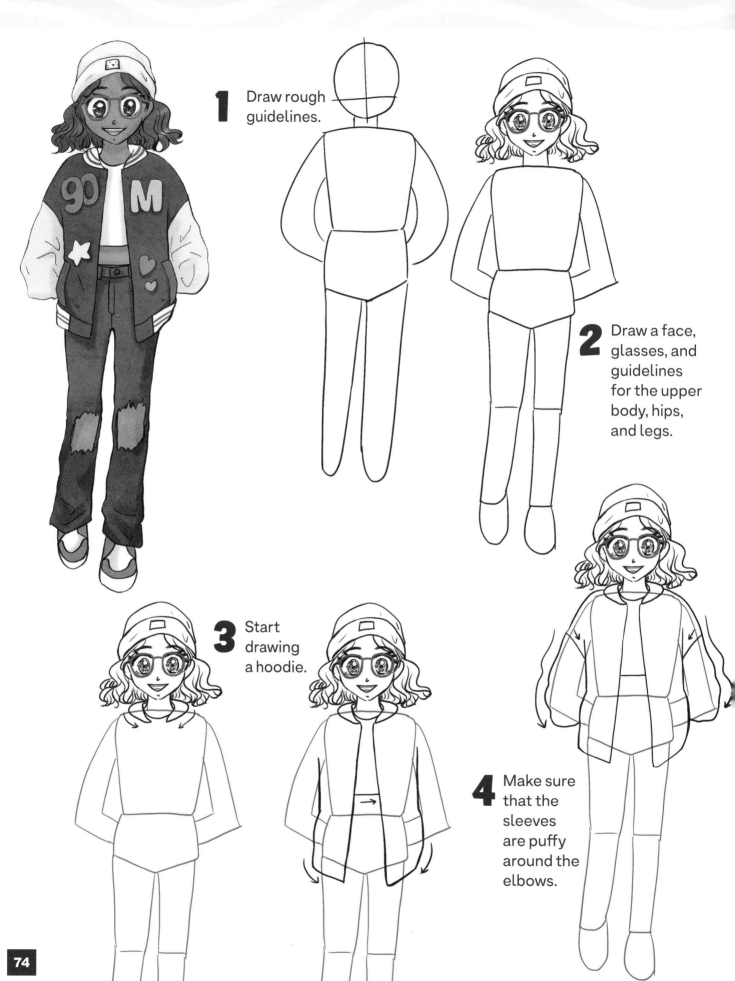

**1** Draw rough guidelines.

**2** Draw a face, glasses, and guidelines for the upper body, hips, and legs.

**3** Start drawing a hoodie.

**4** Make sure that the sleeves are puffy around the elbows.

**5** Draw the belt and zipper.

**6** It's flair jeans! They are baggy and wide. Draw damage holes around the knees. Follow the guide.

**7** Draw shoes that look like raindrops.

**8** Erase the guidelines and draw fabric wrinkles.

**9** Add some colors and patches to the jacket at the end.

90' M

**Misako's note:**
Don't you want to wear cozy outfits in fall?? Let's draw them! This is one of my favorite outfits to draw and wear.

Scan for a video tutorial

**1** Draw rough guidelines.

**2** Draw a face and guidelines for the uppe body, hips, and legs.

**3** Draw a fluffy scarf around her shoulders.

## Misako's note:

Do you like to design dresses? If so, you'll enjoy drawing holiday outfits! Think about dazzling colors and patterns. Let's create one!

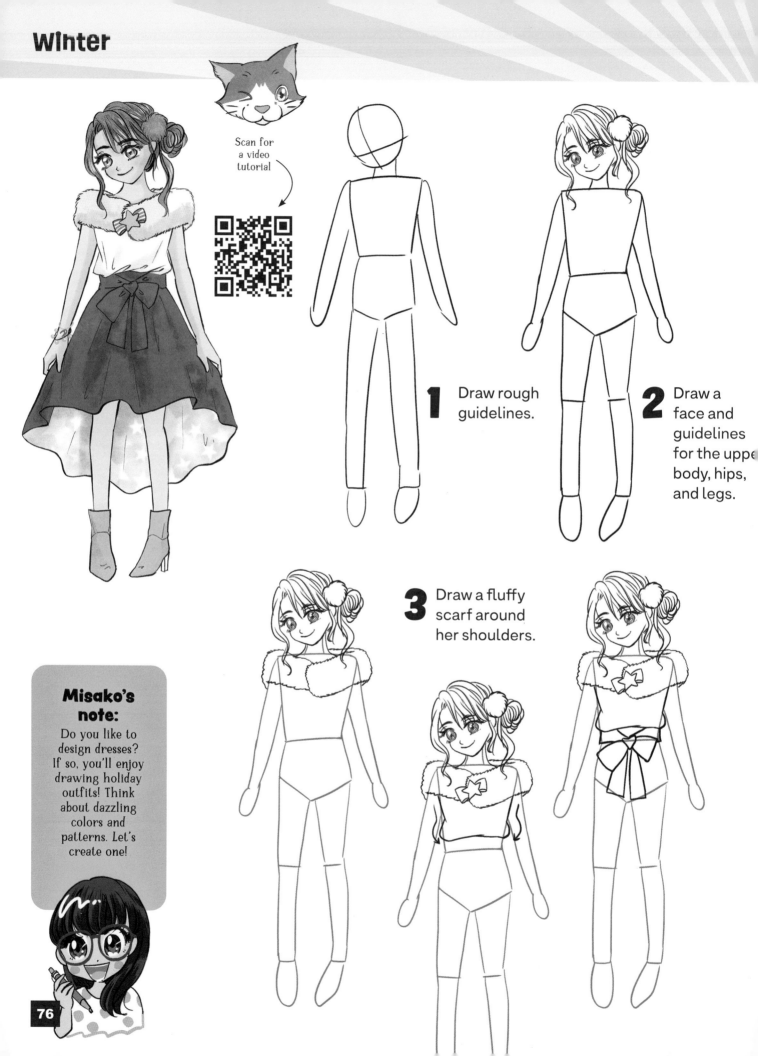

**4** Draw the front of her skirt. It's over-the-knee length.

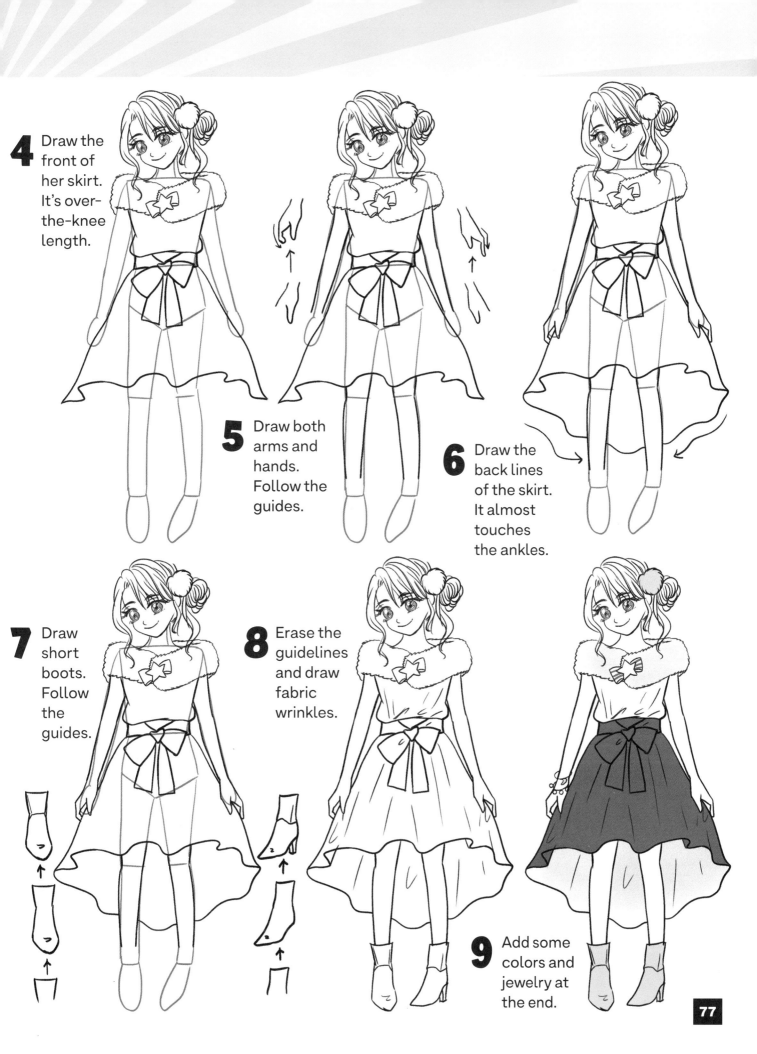

**5** Draw both arms and hands. Follow the guides.

**6** Draw the back lines of the skirt. It almost touches the ankles.

**7** Draw short boots. Follow the guides.

**8** Erase the guidelines and draw fabric wrinkles.

**9** Add some colors and jewelry at the end.

# HARAJUKU ITEMS INSPIRATIONS

FASHION MASK

OVERSIZED HAIR CLIPS

ANIMAL HAT

BOBA TEA

CREPE

ARM WARMERS

ANIMAL BAG

PLATFORM SHOES

**Misako's note:**

Every store in Takeshita Street, which is a well-known area in Harajuku, sells these goodies. It's overwhelming in a good way.

**I drew guidelines for them.
Now you draw their bodies and outfits.**

"I like wearing a street casual outfit for school. It's easy to play sports in this."

"I wear a Harajuku outfit to school all the time! It cheers me up!"

Draw Manga With Misako!

**Misako's note:**
Check out what they're saying and then draw everything!

You can print out more copies to draw with me here!

**LEARN MANGA** *with MISAKO*

# About the Author

**Konnichiwa!**

I am a Japanese manga artist who's published a number of books all over the world. My most recent books are the middle grade graphic novels *Bounce Back* and *No Such Thing as Perfect*. *Bounce Back* was selected to be on the list of 2021 Best Graphic Novels For Children by the American Library Association.

Besides making books, I also teach online manga classes for kids through my online community, Learn Manga with Misako. Please visit my site, www.misakorocks.com.

**Arigato!**